To Lewis and Stewart
With the author's compliments
and every good wish

Denny

Crail 87

BROUGHT UP IN DUBLIN

Brought up in Dublin

DERRY JEFFARES

COLIN SMYTHE
Gerrards Cross 1987

Copyright © 1987 by Derry Jeffares

First published in 1987 by Colin Smythe Limited
Gerrards Cross, Buckinghamshire

British Library Cataloguing in Publication Data
Jeffares, Derry
Brought up in Dublin
I. Title
821'.914   PR6019.E26

ISBN 0-86140-253-7

Produced in Great Britain
Typeset by Crypticks, Leeds,
and printed and bound by Billing & Sons Ltd., Worcester

TO JEANNE

ACKNOWLEDGEMENTS

Acknowledgements are due to the editors of the following in which some of these poems have appeared: *Ariel; Contemporary Review; Etudes Irlandaises* and *Lines Review*.

Contents

THE VILLAGE

Miss Hackett

Miss Hackett kept the village post office
(Had no connection with the Hacketts opposite
Who owned the grocer's shop and public house),
Refused to hand over the keys when held up at night,
Slammed the door on them, then phoned the police.
She was exceedingly cross, precise in her malice,
Had a tin kettle steaming at the ready
And a sister hissing away in a room behind.
She stood upright at her counter, steady,
Alert as a fencer, straight as the state itself,
Guarding the mysteries of its stamp book,
The telephone cabin's black box for pennies,
Gave those wishing to communicate a dirty look.

Timsy

Timsy Hanrahan, handsome man,
Married Agnes, thin-lipped shrew,
Having got her in the family way,
Rebounding from some other girl
Who'd turned him down.
Agnes wore steel-rimmed glasses,
Took a pessimistic view,
Didn't really know what to think
When Timsy took to drink.
They inherited his father's shop
Groceries, papers, sweets and pop,
And coal by the bag or ton.
Timsy drank it all away,
The decent living his father'd won,
Died in a most miserable way,
Rapidly, once consumption had begun;
And Agnes was left, haggard,
Hoarse with shouting at children
Neither of them had wanted.

Mary Irwin

Mary Irwin, wrinkled, kindly,
Limped on her lame leg,
Did great washes on Monday
Rubbing clothes on a scrubbing board.
Filled tin baths with sudsy water,
Talking in her hoarse steamy voice,
Told my mother I'd be an engineer:
'He's that fond of horses'.

Larminie

Larminie was stocky
Sweaty and strong,
Dug the garden for us
With feverish energy,
Smacking the spade down
On what he'd dug and turned,
Chopping worms in half deliberately.
People said it was a pity he was a little wrong
In the head, for he was willing enough
To work when he remembered to come.

Annie

Annie Boyle was shy, uncertain, serious,
Talked at times of her life
In remote Glenmacnass
Where she had never known a stair;
But when her young sister came to stay,
To enjoy a sophisticated holiday,
Told my mother, pityingly,
She was asking where the well was,
The ignorant girl.
Will Boyle, their father, farmed
And was the road mender
From Laragh to Glenmacnass,
Filling the potholes with freestone
From the river bed,
A slow cautious man
Who inclined his head
As he spoke
Carefully.
Annie left us for another post,
But eventually married
And lived in Arklow,
Sent us an occasional letter
Or a postcard
But never told us anything
About the man
She married.

Singleton

Singleton! How did your name arrive,
Forgotten all these years? Peg-leg action
Swinging along, what had you been,
What men and cities had you seen
To give your brown eyes that shrewdness
Under your peaked cap? Your pipe,
Surmounted with fisherman's metal cover,
Had its dottle tapped out on your wooden leg
When you sat alone in the sun by the river.

The Kavanaghs

Molly Kavanagh worked for us.
She was large, had a round freckled face;
Sometimes a puzzled frown gave way
To a lively smile. She talked non-stop.
She married, had children, was happy.
Her father kept pigeons and greyhounds
Behind the cottage with the mud floors
Liable to flooding at times:
The virgin, a red lamp, a hot coalfire,
The steam of drying garments, all clean,
Two rooms, a family of seven:
Religious visions of Heaven.
Old Mrs Kavanagh, talkative too,
Handsome; dark, ravaged face;
Her husband intelligent, sanguine:
Both of them determined to pay their way,
Get their children out of the village.

Suppliers

The delivery men who called had character:
Peter, who whistled as he brought the bread
From a Kennedy's high horse-drawn van,
And asked 'How's the bauld man today?'
Presenting us with a cottage loaf, he said
How good it was. 'Fine and fresh', he began,
Before showing the contents of his wicker basket
He'd selected for appraisal: 'A lovely brack'.
Talked of the weather, his horse's health, his own back,
A rugged faced man, who greatly loved his horse
And was proud of the fresh bread that he brought.

Campbell, the grocer's son, drove their van
(A Chevrolet, grey with cheery wooden orange wheels)
Cap-aslant, brisk: 'How's the young man?'
These rituals were observed, as in their shop
His father offered biscuits from a glass-topped tin
Once my mother's ordering had come to a stop.

For some strange reason I can't remember
What on earth we got from the rich chocolate
Of a van, gilt-lettered 'Boileau and Boyd
Manufacturing chemists', the driver and mate
Known to me as 'Mr Boil – oh and Mr Boyd'.
Quite pleased they were at their promotion
To Huguenot and Scottish names, their smart white coats
Matching the glossy polished panels of their van.

Opposite us stood a shop, the Milltown Spirit Stores.
We seldom bought anything there: groceries to the right
And on the left capped men spitting on the floor,
Sawdust thinly spread: a Guinness in their right,
A pipe in their left hand, and the dark melancholy
Of drawn porter oppressing the sour heavy air.

It changed hands; an alert keen-faced man called Croke
Bustled about in a long ochre coat doing his best,
But bothered by his wife's frail health. She had no zest,
No energy, and when even mild waves of fate broke

18

About her she surrendered at once, was swept away,
And James Croke's once bright face grew ashen grey.
He couldn't make a go of it; it simply didn't pay,
He told my father. Secretly I thought him poisoned
By the rancid air that filled the gloomy shop,
By the dismal life behind it coming to a stop.

The real reason poor Croke couldn't succeed
Was that another shop more fully met the village need,
And it was down the hill in the middle of the street
Where the village lived, an ugly concrete building,
Tomas O h'Acaid on the front, in faded gilding;
Within, a partition divided off the groceries;
Beyond the hatch dim faces, glasses, shuffling feet . . .
The Hackett brothers extended credit to the village
And, some people said, combined supply with pillage,
Being called gombeen men behind their calculating backs.

Shivaun

Shivaun, scarlet-faced with rage,
Was a termagent
Hard to fathom,
Till my parents realised
She drank
And stole,
Had filled cases
With everything
She could lay her hands on
When they were out.

1924

Ticking of the Raleigh's three speed; and he was there
Radiating delight, asking us what we'd done,
Telling of his day, his blue eyes and fair hair
Scintillating in the rays of an afternoon sun.

In those days he'd leave the office early enough
To help my mother to push me most of the way
Up Dartry Hill in the go-cart, filled with picnic stuff,
His rod, fishing bag and toys with which I'd play
On the broad green bank while he cast his flies
Dexterously, line snaking out over deep pool
Where brown water swirled and trout would rise,
Many of tolerable size brought to land, the spool
Of the reel winding speedily, and supper assured.

The Dodder fed a mill stream and it slid, leisured,
Sinister, dark below sycamores, an artificial channel
Guiding its power beneath stone bridge into a tunnel
And the rushing noise behind the walls of neat dye works
Built on the side of a steep hill, name written in gold
Round a clock, clean lorries in ochre and olive green.

Somewhere still in that four-year-old memory there lurks
The smell of trout cooking when we got home, images untold
Of the circling of dragon flies under the trees, or the quick flick
Minnows make at the threat of a child's thrown stick,
Excursions into wonder; though not much more than a mile
From Elm Grove House: all exciting enough to file away:
Effects, cumulative, of each timeless greening day.

Ascendancy

'Dirty protestant', he shouted
When I was surrounded.
He was gap-toothed, carrot-haired,
Snotty-nosed, six inches taller,
In command of seven or eight
Equally menacing.

Only a hundred and fifty yards
From Donegan's shop to home;
But that lay round the corner,
Up the hill. And I was
Surrounded.

I had been sent on a message,
Was clutching some parsley,
Had never known hatred before,
And found it inexplicable,
As well as terrifying.

Someone had seen them
And shouted something.
I thought I was lucky
To get away with a split lip,
To get away at all,
Up the hill.

ENVIRONS OF DUBLIN

Milltown Road

Before the buses came we'd half a mile to walk
Down Milltown's country road, innocent of tar,
Its grassy banks dusted as if by white chalk,
The fine road dust. It almost was too far
This distance, once we'd gone beyond the fields,
Passing a terrace of six houses with balconies,
Narrow gateway leading to the garden that shields
Their privacy from passer's glance. Opposite rise
Twin flights of granite steps to Greenmount's door,
Then the pierced iron gates, the door in the wall
Of Grove House where some artist or illustrator
Built a third storey, a simple room, perched tall
Above the roof, an aircraft carrier's superstructure.
Next massive wooden gates, the farm of Milltown Park,
And the high granite-walled road's long curvature
Winds dully along its bend, gloomy and dark
Until the last open stretch, past St James's drive
To the crossroads, where, on the last of the double lines,
An eleven tram, inert, waits for its fellow to arrive
Clattering down single line that led from twin sheds,
Where all the trams, I was told, had their beds,
Their trolleys wound down at night, the day's work done.
The eleven was a dull route, its only thrill,
After the rush along the narrow, leafy Appian way,
Leeson Street bridge, where the lock might be ready to fill
For some turf barge pulled by a patient horse.

D.S.E.R.'s Bray and Greystones

Number 434 was a 2-4-2,
A high-funnelled high-domed tank;
Crammed on its footplate we went through
All stations to Bray, possessing a permit
Officially signed. The crew were given a tip;
We stood on the platform, watching passengers exit,
Tank engine chuff off, come back on centre track,
Be coupled up, then leave with wheels aslip,
Spinning wildly until they found some grip
And the train vanished off out of our view.

We waited there for the Greystones train to come,
Got chocolate from a most antique machine,
At last heard the engine clanking up the line,
A 4-4-0, lithe and handsome,
With inside cylinders, six foot driving wheels,
An express engine, clearly come down in the world.
She left the turntable, was coupled to the train,
Tender to the front, while the driver unfurled
A battered roll of canvas from the top of the cab,
Explaining that this would restrain the rain,
The continuous rain of drops from the tunnel tops,
And Greystones had only a thirty-two foot turntable,
And he had to take this train back to Dublin,
So the engine should face forward on the way back.

We started, swung left where the single line overtips
The surrounding roads, then a cutting, a halt unable
To justify itself at Naylor's Cove, the line risen
Above sea level, abandoned tunnel showing where the track
Was driven back by the sea's fierce eroding force.
We entered the tunnels, one bored in nineteen-seventeen,
Eleven hundred yards, light dancing from open firebox,
Loud battering noise echoing, harsh, from black rocks
Resounding till, regulator eased, we were descending
To Greystones, up platform. We took on water there
Brought the engine down the line, backed up, sea air
Whipping the smoke away as she ran light, reversed
To the carriages, and off.

                    Now we were able to peer
At Ram's Scalp Bridge, accident site where joint gave
Between the bridge rail and a new bullhead, bending
As a passenger train from Enniscorthy crashed sheer
Over the bridge that spanned the Brandy Hole
A hundred feet below; there smugglers used to run
Their cargoes where fast-flowing streams lave
The rocks, racing to the sea. This fatal caracole
Left engine and tender bottom up, carriages overrun,
The last overhanging the platform of the wooden bridge
Propped by the semi-upright gutted floor of another:
Two dead, twenty-three injured in the smother
Of telescoped stock, flying debris, falling rock,
On an August day in eighteen sixty-seven.

Afterwards we talked more of railway accidents,
Through the engine's hissing steam at Bray,
Discussed the spectacular one of nineteen hundred.
A goods engine's wheels locked on greasy rails;
Reversing failed to slow it, train slid like a sledge,
The fireman jumped clear, the buffer stops gave way,
The engine burst through retaining wall; hung high
Over Hatch Street but, most surprisingly, didn't fall.
The driver, William Hyland, gave evidence in hospital:
'At Ranelagh I applied the vacuum brake, reversed her
As we passed the stationmaster's office; she never stopped'.
(My mother had a photograph of the engine propped there
Looking incongruous, cantilevered out in the air).

Sandwiches eaten, watch examined, signal dropped,
We eased the train out of Bray, and clattered on our way
Shrilly whistling, crossing points at Shanganagh Junction,
Then slowed to a stop at Shankill, next at Foxrock,
Then Stillorgan and Dundrum, some conjunction
Of shared ideas leading to a fine head of steam
And a rousing sixty reached on the downhill,
On the straight to Milltown, stopped with scream
Of locked wheels, well beyond the platform,
All delighted we'd exceeded any suburban norm,

Let that gallant old lady, number 60, have her fun.
Next morning, pulling out of Milltown, she'd barely begun
To move her train, then threw her nearside connecting rod.

Dublin Buses

Cross the road, stand outside the dark glass –
Three Victorian coloured bottles in the chemist's shop –
Let the blue and yellow Tramway bus pass,
Wait for the smaller, closely following red *Robin*
To swerve towards the path and lurch to a stop,
Driver blipping the International's rorty sounding
Clapped-out engine, haze and reek of tired old oil
Seeping past gearbox gaiter and gaps in floorboards,
Passengers bracing themselves as we begin
To chase the blue and yellow rival, bounding
Over cobbled tram tracks, the pursuit a turmoil
Of effort until passing the other bus briefly affords
Our driver a smile, since he will pick up the next knot
Of waiting passengers. It is a boy's adventure yarn
This daily, epic struggle for passengers; whether or not
Passing made any change in what each bus would earn
On the whole journey, the violent rivalry could burn
So deeply that the private *Robin* company ran two buses
At a time, leap-frogging past their rival in turn –
All to no ultimate avail. For after protests, fusses
About reckless driving, the aggressive *Robins* vanished
    finally;
The Dundrum route became the property of the D.U.T.C.
Four Dennis buses each with a distinct personality
Then kept time, with uniformed conductors, drivers set apart,
Cab over the bonnet, their actions only to be perceived
By twisting round on rear-facing seat – whence the art
Of doubledeclutching was learned, how gears behaved,
And the effect of the long handbrake pushed forward,
Hard, to slow the heavy, clumsy monsters down.
Five past the hour we expected 337
To climb the hill, erratic, performance uneven
Compared to others; 338, with rearward
Grace of cut-out door, made her way to town
At twenty past the hour, often late, while 336,
At twenty five to, seemed by far the fastest of the four;
339, my favourite, also with cut-out door,
Completed the programme; and by her one could fix
The time precisely, ten minutes to the hour.

Unpredictable maroon buses ground up to Enniskerry,
Low-geared ADCs mostly, eminently memorable
For wheezing and groaning, called *The Wicklow Hills*,
Lasting interminably until finally swallowed by C.I.E.
Then there were buses which rattled and clattered
Their decrepit way to Churchtown until the state
Forced mergers (and this surely not a day too late).
One fourteen-seater Chevrolet joined *The General*
(Proprietor L. E. McNally), not yet so battered
As the rest of that fleet; it seemed peripheral
To the company since its former owner shared driving
With his former employee. They drove philosophically,
Courteous to passengers, smiling at schoolboys arriving
Beside them to open and shut the folding front door.
Their pointed shoes as greasy as the pedals and floor,
They broke the law contentedly, constantly, never stranding
Passengers who crammed in gratefully, standing,
Then lurching, as the topheavy, overbodied, overloaded
Vehicle rolled its way, carefully dodging the bumps
All known by heart by passengers as well as drivers.

Pirate buses used to operate occasionally,
Choosing what seemed a lucky time and route
In those hectic twenties' days of free enterprise
Before Bigger meant a loss of small-scale personal loot.
The flair that had painted many saints' names
In flowing script on buses of generally small size
Gives way to numbers which Tramway emblem frames
First on the deep blue sides, then on aluminium, next on grey
Then on light green, after on pleasing darker green.
C.I.E. favoured country reds and city blue and yellow
(Deriving from the former I.O.C. and G.N.R.;
The latter's Gardiner-engined thirty-five seaters
Smelt of scented disinfectant blown through their heaters);
Now on Bombadiers a sophisticated scheme of green
Replaces the sickly gamboge, old gold, on Van Hools,
Clumsy double deckers, thus making a medley the fools
Would have approved, blindly, in Swift's Laputa land.

The Citroën

Boanerges, our son of Thunder, with distinctive note
of straight cut gears, aptly named banjo case
with gap-toothed crown wheel, and so remote
from modern transport, was a car with its own face,
and personality: when in the mood it sought to please,
bowling along at a resounding, steady forty-five.
Sometimes it could simply sulk, or successfully tease,
twice boiling its water away climbing the Rocky Valley,
bursting two high pressure tyres in one drive,
spewing hot oil from its vertical dashboard gauge
on white flannels. Its temperament made each journey
a hazardous expedition, creating intense pleasure or rage
in us who sat often frozen in the narrow steel torpedo body
of that Citroën 11.4 tourer, our first car.

The coasts of Dublin and Wicklow, with the melody
of incoming waves, were exposed by it for exploration.
The inland rivers and mountains, all the woody
nooks of the Coronation Plantation, the fine obscuration
of small roads in County Meath, weekend after weekend,
we got to know them well. My mother would sometimes
bring my sister and myself, perhaps a friend or two,
for a picnic after school. Up the twists and climbs
of Ballinascorney Gap, Ticknock or Hell Fire Club
she would sling the Citroën with eclat, would send
it nosing up lanes (rocky tracks my father would avoid)
until turning at the more than ultimate end she'd rub
running boards or long wings against some gate
or loose granite wall, dash downhill again to town
to get to Merrion Square, and avoid being late
to bale my father out of his dull office by five,
wearing her leather coat, her black and white hat,
her long gauntlets; she looked dashingly alive.

Then

Space and time are what matter most;
Extend the one, the other stretches too.
This clear truth subconsciously I knew,
Felt as a child the ignominy of the zoo
With its pacing tigers, sea-lions in their pool,
Yaks and buffaloes mouching forlorn,
Drab in concrete railed-in yard. No movement,
For they'd no space to get up speed, had sent
Their thoughts beyond constraining time.
Our luck was better. Rocking on its stiff springs
Train behind 2-4-2 tank would slowly climb
Up from Milltown along the straight to Dundrum,
Leopardstown, Foxrock and then Carrickmines.
Into Bray on late spring afternoons we used to come,
Walk to the esplanade, below it the empty strand,
Paddle, swim, build castles and tunnels in the sand,
Soothed by the brimming space of the boundless sea
Until my father came by the Westland Row train,
Shedding the thought of town. Then both our parents swam,
And time's ritual continued with picnic tea,
Cornish pasties or sandwiches, and, to entertain,
Their contents were clad in mystery until we ate.
When the sun vanished, the air grew chill
And time intruded once more as it grew late;
But the space extended it, back to the station,
Then the inland vistas stretched it further still,
And back we came, achievement in our ennervation;
The enclosing space of the house held time's invitation
To tour its ample void, endurable in sleep's standstill.

Chapelizod

Now burglar alarms ring round the suburb
Where larks and corncrakes used to make a din.
Why should three bedroomed semis so disturb
The peace, scatter the rear of darkness thin?
What have they to attract young breakers-in?
The telly perhaps, or video? What else can show
A green light of envy to unemployed eye?
Ah, there's the rub, the young are high.

The Birds

Ascal o' néanacáin, avenue of the birds;
And so indeed it proved to be. Hedges, trees
And the hills beyond a living sanctuary.
A wild duck brought eight ducklings at dawn
Into our garden pond, where herons stole the fish;
The corncrakes rattled through those sleepy fields,
Fat missel thrushes ate the berries of Italian oak.
Chaffinches and bluetits, wrens and blackbirds,
Thrushes and an occasional willy wagtail
Bustled about the place, their song a happy medley,
Larks, too, and a covey of partridge once appeared . . .
Yes, you will say, why all this Richard Jefferies stuff?
In part the country nature of the city, the Pillar
Twenty minutes away by bicycle, given a following wind;
In part the change I registered there last year,
With concrete roads, estates and lines of shops
Offering suburban uniformity . . . the past was for the birds.

SCHOOLS

Selskar

Miss Flynn, thirty, wore shiny Russian boots
And a red cloche hat, taught us music,
Draped herself elegantly as though shoots
And tendrils climbed close round the thick
Stalk of the piano stool. So very romantic
Her powder, lipstick and long cigarette holder,
Her soft white fingers caressing the keys:
Withdrawn, amused at our efforts to please,
She seemed a being come from another world,
Unlike sandy-haired Miss Marion, Scotch and plain,
Her hair turning grey with the constant strain
Of agreeing so deprecatingly, as she furled
Her umbrella, about the unpleasant driving rain
Or any other bone Miss Moorhead threw to her
For crunching conversation. She knew her place
And this was written clearly across her patient face,
For Miss Moorhead dictated when talk could recur,
Made it so clear Miss Marion was employed by her.

Miss Marion taught the youngest spelling and tables
Cats sitting on mats, hor-ses in the sta-bles
Twice two is five and all that sort of thing.
Miss Moorhead took the seniors, teaching
Geography, places where Irish rivers were reaching
Into the sea, out of date statistics about trade,
Where Guinness was brewed, or Jacobs biscuits made;
And History, why London's tower made princes afraid,
How round towers resisted many a Danish raid;
And Copybook Writing, full of moral maxim and adage
Which Miss Moorhead most sternly applauded,
Since by sheer hard work and no one defrauded
(Except Miss Marion on her insecure starvation wage)
She'd built her clientele up, knowing to her advantage
Ranelagh, Palmerston Park, Donnybrook and Rathgar
Protestant catchment areas, named her school Selskar
After the Wexford she came from and hankered for,
Living with her shapeless sister in a Clonskeagh terrace,
The river Dodder almost running by their back door.

Miss Weaver, Stella, taught gym, her young face
Pink above dark blue gym dress, serious on the job,
Blushing shyly but moving us round with skill,
Carefully watching us, ordering us to bend and bob,
To skip and run. Drill came to a sweaty stand-still,
Shoes were changed, benches moved back from the walls,
The framed texts showed again. There was goodwill
On the platform where the staff (all three) sipped down tea
(Kettle on gas ring in washroom outside the lavatory)
And we could leave our places with time to fill
With talk while we ate our sandwiches, drank milk
And slowly got to know each other: Gerry Rowe,
Smart boy; Theo Dunne with golden hair like silk;
Adorable Evelyn Griffin, the older girl I got to know
Who made bootees of lace for my black cat to wear,
Though that outraged animal's first act was to tear
Them off against the garden wall; Raymond Short
Became my friend despite his loathsome sport
Of pulling wings off flies; there was the Dowd family,
A severe sister, two raw-boned brothers with thick skins;
And Herbert Plant whose mother was reputed, slimily,
To plaster his hair with oil from sardine tins.
I can't remember any others, can't envisage anymore
Than the coloured glass porch, Selskar School, above the door.
Not true. My subconscious has tried to bury the concert,
The annual showing off to parents: a spelling bee,
Songs and recitations, all intended to divert,
To please. But I had learned 'Bad Sir Brian Botany',
Was announced by mistake, told to sit down again;
Later, tensed, climbed the platform, made a mess of it,
Jumbling the verses, word-order, stood uncertain,
Silent there till my father's whisper came explicit
From the third row of chairs. 'Take a deep breath,
And begin again'. The second attempt went successfully
Though I felt someone else reciting instead of me.
Yes, that confusion I do remember: my red hot face
And what seemed a sea of grinning faces filling the space,
The mysterious dark confusion beyond the platform,
On which I felt I'd made an exhibition of myself

38

By failing to cope with the unexpected, failing to perform,
Failing to do justice to the patient training
My father had given me, to make me recite
Without the rhythm of 'the boy stood on the burning deck'
The place where I had stood that flaming night!

Headmaster of the High School

We weren't, it was known, taught grammar well
Nor the writing of Greek and Latin verse
But we read voraciously so many authors
(The *Vera Historia* beckons me to try Lucian again)
Not on any syllabus. We heard you intersperse
Anecdotes of life in Trinity in nineteen-ten
When the young dons were lively bachelors
And walked with pupils where alps glisten
Still (but no one goes to read) sure all was well
In Edwardian peace, that no one need listen
For the distant rumbling of the avalanche.
Through you we learned of Arnoldian rapture
Muted later by the lino, perversely painted graining,
Sepia photographs of the Coliseum that capture
What was lost: an ability confidently to launch
Your boat on the river and then without straining
Follow the current – till the boat grounded
Here on the mud flats where there sounded
Every forty-five minutes the clanging bell
Outside the Clockroom, then down in the yard.
No tide rose to sweep you free from that bell's spell,
From routine chores. On the breeze, when the doors
Closed on the sixth form, came a faint backward
Whiff of what Horace had meant to you, and still meant,
And later, teaching Greek to three boys, you leant
Forwards with delight, holding a paper against the light
On which you'd drawn something we couldn't see –
Such was your pleasure we could but agree
As if we understood Thucydides' account of Sicily,
The awful avalanche Alcibiades caused there,
When really all you conveyed was your deep love
Of classical authors, your memories of the blue above
Those timeless, healthy Alpine reading parties.

H. R. Chillingworth
(*Times* Correspondent on Education in Ireland)

Eating cucumber sandwiches
From a black tin box,
Gown flowing as breeze pitches
In and out, unlocks
The Greek key pattern as you walk
Alone, not wishing to talk
Or share ideas with any others,
Blue eyes sharply recording sunshine,
Roundly matching the fine line
Of your nose, the outdoor red
Of cheeks, the bright clear white
Of hair and moustache, boots black,
Grey flannel suit beneath the gown,
All elegant but unsuited to town
Even to the subsequent puzzled frown
At how our attention grew slack,
How we failed to share any delight
In the chores of phonetics,
Not realising, despite what you said,
That you were equally bored
With all school French could afford.

Brown wistful eyes, set a little too close,
A high-pitched Cork voice; in everything brisk,
Precise, he taught us to avoid the otiose,
To plan, to cover the course, avoid the risk
Of an unprepared answer – for efficiency
Was his watchword, though he could talk
About his exciting times in Persia, if encouraged.

We were impressed when we first saw him walk
A racing bicycle through the gate, then outraged
When he first imposed his most rigid discipline
Since we had been used to a far milder rule,
A gentlemanly approach to literature, the sanguine
Predictability of Butler's English teaching. A fool
If but well-mannered received from him no derisive snorts
(Kildare land and golf beckoned him to desired retirement,
The Kildare Street Club could well have been his habitat)
But this new man, seen riding his bicycle in shorts,
Was young and forceful, and hints of an exotic scent
Hung metaphorically about him, still bronzed after Isphafan.

He lived alone high up in a Dawson Street attic flat;
From the shelves there a few of us reading History began
To receive books on loan, skilfully selected. He was out
To question our ideas, extend the range of our thought:
We heard how he had entered Trinity as a brilliant Sizar
In Science, next got a Scholarship in History and ought
To have gone on to a First, but, in gesture spectacular,
Exchanged books in his last year with a friend reading Persian,
Sat Moderatorship and got the price of his conceit, a Third.
What could he do but use this useless oriental degree
To teach abroad, to hide himself in a Persian mystery?
The roses remained for ever fresh in his memory,
And for ever, too, the *Gulistan's* moral thoughts of Sa'adi.

Later he bandaged the wound, indeed acted the physician,
Grafted on a Ph.D. in English – and now could gird
At one and all who failed to redeem a mistake,
Since he had demonstrated what could still be done,

That he could cover up his youthful vanity, remake
A broken career. He married, had children, then won
A Headmastership, became most benign, died young.

The Staff

Names of the staff were so obvious:
Sammy, Chas, Willy, Watty, Jack,
Welsh Pointy (because of the way he made a fuss
'You boy, stand up there, yes, you at the back')
Jumbo Simpson, too, and Chilly-Bom-Bom,
Boozie Butler, indeed, and Froggy Young . . .
One name, however, that had not rung
Any bell in a mind precociously well read
In school stories and thus ready for 'Beak'
Was a traditional name allotted to the Head
(Unsuitable, too, for his usual gentleness)
Of Bear – though when under stress
A sudden temper could tear and tweak
His soft Cork accent into depths and heights
Of vibrancy. All of them were irritable,
It seemed; by the end of term liable
To irrational rage, caught in some cage
Where boys could daily stare at them
As behind the bars they paced the strip
Of annual Inter, Leaving and Sizarship.

The Bell

At ten to three the anticipated clanging bell.
Permission – to sprint down stairs, through hall,
Tumble down wooden outside stairs to a narrow yard,
Past Imrie's room, turn then and run hard
Across the main yard's cobbles to the shed,
Fire books into the bag and pedal to the steps,
Then lift, up, and walk to the gate that led
To freedom. Past Harcourt Street station
Over the stone setts of Camden Street, then the canal,
Through Ranelagh's fading gentility, banal
In shabby faded stucco, palms and gamboge brick
To more modern reds, past walls curving thick
In the solidity of granite, border of Milltown Park,
And home, sheltering behind the elder hedge's dark,
The large green door, scents of the hidden garden,
And the sure welcome, the exchange of views,
Something delicious to eat, *Irish Times* to peruse
Before accepting the Dublin mountains' invitation
To explore the quarried newt pools on Ticknock
Beyond Lamb Doyle's, to dream of restoration
Of a ruined farmhouse shell, eighteen-fifteen
Carved on the door's lintel, that massive block
Of granite. And, beneath, all Dublin Bay seen
As if from an aircraft, ultramarine blue, serene
In the clear scented air, all the colours there pure,
White rocks sparkling in the fresh sunlight,
Viridian lines of trees and hedges standing as sure
Protectors of boundaries on the hillside, giving a right
To privacy, making it so well worth the afternoon climb
To escape from that school bell's control of time.

Sergeant Nelson

Sharp waxed ends to his white moustache;
Frosty blue eyes that had looked on Spion Kop
Could be used, coldly, to quell the brash,
But as time went on he seemed to thaw,
And on his rounds, calling out to defaulters
'Youse boys to see the Headmaster at one o'clock',
We realised he bore no malice; we saw
Him as part of the accepted encounters
Between teachers and taught, lock, stock
And barrel of the hierarchical rule we had to serve,
Though later, as six formers allowed within his box,
We began to understand his strength of nerve,
The bravery, the discipline, the hard knocks
That made him, Frosty, a most respected friend.

Too Far

Further off lay Kippure, dour Djouce
All too apt to be cloudcapped;
Mullaghcleevaun or Tonalagee
Much further still, too far for me
On a bicycling expedition
With obligatory homework waiting.
Within Time's easier limits
Lay the twisting valley of Glencullen
Or the Featherbed and Sallygap,
But too far the mysterious sullen
Deep legendary Lough Nanighan
With its monster menacingly waiting –
Damnable, doubtless, like the homework.

School Tie

The boy who sat beside me for a year
Constantly showed off the thickness
Of his wrists. Once he brought me near
To death, as near as I've ever been,
By pulling my tie impossibly tight
So I could not breathe, and the fear
Of breathlessness is with me yet, the fright
That he did not realise, had not seen
That he must help to undo the knottiness
His strong wrists had firmly tightened
From behind me, as I looked out of the window
At some thin-wristed boys playing below.

Junior Exhibition

A summer Saturday afternoon for Junior Exhibition,
Those *eau-de-Nil* walls reflecting scratching pens
(For we used real ink in those pre-biro days
In flexible Waverley nibs or harsher Js).
Missing the rally of vintage cars at Donnybrook
While translating Don Ciochete from the Irish
Seemed, under these conditions, simply brutish;
No labour of love; nothing culture-vulturish
In earning a university education by examination.

FAMILY

Professor McDowell

The earliest McDowell I know
Was a case of academic vanity,
The fatal lure of wanting to show
Ability to play the man of action.
He came from a Papal bull-begotten
Ancient sottish Scottish university;
The first professor of Philosophy
Set upon a chair in Groningen,
He set himself to the redaction
Of his writings in the Latin tongue,
Instructed the stolid students there
In logic, all the philosophical fare
Thought suitable for the local young,
Until he was recruited as an agent,
Became important, King Charles's man,
And the tragedy of his life began.

He was, of course, successful at first,
But languished later in Rotterdam,
In the squalid gaol, hydroptic thirst
For further philosophy come too late.
Cromwell wanted him handed over
When the Treaty was ready, the slate
About to be wiped clean, his cover
Obviously now completely blown.

After the Restoration he appears again,
'The man McDowell', who has grown
Into a suppliant for some reward
For all that hardship, when he'd lain
Bereft in Rotterdam, health broken.
The State Papers increasingly afford
Less space to him, who had spoken
Of his hopes, indeed become a bore,
Trying to get his foot within the door
By sliding piteous petitions under it.
And then he ceases to be mentioned,

Died in great want, no doubt, and without
Any royalties from those books he wrote.

William McDowell

Tibradden mountain or Barnaculla,
Ballinascorney Gap, Ticknock, the Scalp,
Enniskerry, Stepaside and Kilternan,
Some of these names I found most romantic
As a schoolboy, when rustic Templeogue
Had its steam tram, and the dark Dodder
Ran past Oldbawn's stonecrusher. In Firhouse
Great-grandfather McDowell's house still stands,
Surrounded by new buildings; but he was cozened
Out of it, Irish Willie, who deep in Carlisle
Stewarded an estate, ran away to Gretna Green
With the daughter, and married her in the Forge
Before her enraged father caught up with them,
To reward the elopement that stuck in his gorge
With banishment to Ireland (which he abhorred),
Offsetting her loss of ancestral land with a tilery
And a fat farm outside the town of Tipperary.

There they prospered, lived happily until she died.
They though it no harm, having liberated themselves,
To send two daughters unchaperoned to Baden Baden
To flirt with German officers; it was a matter of pride
They should be educated properly (from her shelves
My grandmother took a German dictionary, translated
An essay – accurately – for me when she was a hundred).
Both daughters returned and married their Irishmen.
Alone, McDowell came to Dublin to his house
To be nearer his daughters; how it was unfunded
Was a mystery: my mother thought him betrayed,
Spoke mainly of the style in which he had lived
And the magnificent garden in which she played
Before some related lawyer's shady tricks deprived
Him of his money, took away his house – but failed to rouse
His ire; for he remained the most gentle of men,
Whitebearded, an entertainer of children by the fire.

A Wild Great-Uncle

To walk where molten Vesuvius flowed
Is to recall the past in a form perturbing,
To think how the force beneath bellowed,
Erupted up its sulphurous violence, disturbing
All in its path, wild rage imposing its will.

Great-uncle Wattie was no longer stirred
By choleric fits; indeed his appearance belied
Past anecdotes: clear blue-eyed, white-whiskered –
Yet there was evidence here of the man who'd terrified
Children, treating nieces and nephews as he had his own,
For, in his prime, if anyone had irritated him
Even though the cause of his rage was unknown
He'd erupt, fling a plate at them, loaded to the brim,
Roaring madly if it shattered on wall or floor
While his wife summoned a maid by her bell,
Murmuring gently to him: 'Wattie, no more,
That's enough, no more', indicating where the mess fell
To the maid trained for such tantrums.

                                    Enough indeed
To prove him a true Bates, a wild Meath man, and more,
A rich farmer, like his brothers, who liked to breed
Racehorses as well as ranch fat cattle galore.
He and his brother John had gambled, ridden madly –
John, blinded by a branch as he jumped a ditch,
Faced his fate stoically and completely unsadly,
Farmed on, considered a good judge of a beast,
Lived a batchelor, liked plump girls on his knee,
Went to the races, got royally drunk most regularly,
Stumbling back to Killeglands after some spree,
An ashplant his only guide. The other brother,
Willie, despite his masculine beard, was weaker,
It was widely known that any woman would smother
His will. His wife's companion was chief speaker
Over the silver tea set; her Scottish pertinacity
Easily extracted whatever money had remained
After an easy threesome, remarkable for its opacity,
Broke apart, and sale of Rollestown was put in train.

Baltrasna, Wattie's father's house, lay vacant
In the centre of their land; at haymaking
Wattie and a holidaying nephew sat inelegant
In its old kitchen eating sandwiches, slaking
Field-thirsts with Guinness brought from a wooden crate.
It was a long thatched house in a good state,
Its thick whitewashed walls completely appropriate,
Insulating it beneath that broad Meath sky
From heat and cold alike. I still wonder why
Wattie let his wife drive him out of living there –
I suppose she wanted to tame him, to domesticate
Those erupting, earth-shaking rages, may have been aware
That a stone house could contain them, civilise
Her wild man whom she loved. Her own refinement
Deprecated the countryman that he remained in town
(Marvelling at the vast amount of money he'd spent
In the Shelbourne, but paying up without a frown).
Wryly she humoured him; as if, peering over the crater's rim,
She feared his primitive force. And, somewhat loath,
He humoured her, somewhat to her faint surprise,
Left Baltrasna (which she called a mud hut) for Ratoath,
For Glebelands, a stone rectory closed in by trees.

One son died: a room filled with motor magazines
Acted as his shrine; the second let Canada freeze
His affection cold; only Ida saw changing scenes,
New gentleness creeping in as his age advanced;
She could control his movements and her mother's,
Using her driving skills, as her Singer Nine pranced
Along the dusty roads, her will now smoothing his pothers,
Leaving him for his half one, and often several more,
At the village pub, before he strode back for dinner,
Not domesticated yet at eighty, cleaned the bore
Of a single barrelled gun, and was the winner
Of yet another round, arriving with a dead bird
In his wife's elegant dining room, to her cry of 'Absurd'.
Absurd he may indeed have been, but to a young child
Walking over the pumice dust of his raging past
He seemed latently explosive, still dangerously wild.

Hamiltons

The Hamilton cousins were a whiff of the jazz age,
Hearty and healthy, as outspoken as you'd find,
Off to race meetings or to whatever was the rage:
Dances, cocktail parties, midnight treasure hunts,
Or else shooting or fishing or swimming, their cars aligned
Outside Lake Park at Lough Dan covered in white dust,
Vee-radiatored Armstrong Siddeley tourers. But the mud
Is what I remember, when something created a flood
At their town house, in Raheny, *rus in urbe* by the sea:
There they seemed Olympians, called their father Bud,
Went their dashing ways, drank, smoked, swore with audacity,
Willoughby known as Rat, Blayney and the lovely Mavis,
Twenties girl, assured and poised whatever she did.
The house was littered with signs of sport; tennis
Or badminton racquets, golf clubs, bats, croquet mallets –
Stage properties, indeed the house a stage for candid
Chaffing noisy bonhomie, spectacular exits and entries,
Swirling, intense yet casual. Mavis put me on her horse
Which dashed off madly. 'Very good job you ducked',
She said, after the brute shot off under an arch,
Then deposited me, having completed its wild course
Round the grounds. Their mother, extremely kind,
Survived, happily, by ignoring all their nonsenses,
Detached, interested in her guinea fowl – 'Stupidest of habits,
They panic, strangle themselves in my wire fences' –
She had cages of red-eyed munching angora rabbits,
Dogs, cats, animals galore, and all hyper-active.
'Tiny, your wife looks tired, a rest will do her good;
We're away, use the house, the servants will do the food.'

Births, Deaths and Marriages

Crumbling headstones speak with gentle affection
Of wives or husbands, show the tight connection
Of cousins – Sealys, Boxwells, Letts and Sparrows.

Marriage bonds knit the Jeffares to these few families
And the big family Bible, not often read for its homilies,
Recorded all the details of this interbreeding.

My Aunt Ada, not liking her own age to be known,
Flew into a passion once, in almighty rage
Tore out and burnt up every single page.

Devoted Mothers

I still feel angry when I recollect
How my father, offered a contract by La Scala
At seventeen, felt the powerful effect
Of Edwardian possessiveness: a heart attack
Threatened by his widowed mother,
Who, like Mrs Synge, just three roads away,
Attended Zion Church, wanted to smother
Anything artistic. Mrs Synge was sure
Musicians were not nice: besides, they drank.

TRINITY

Reading Room

Decorous flirtations, signs of going steady,
Were to be observed in the Reading Room gallery –
If one had time to lift one's head from the pages
Of Liddell and Scott, or was it Lewis and Short?
The click of high heels, the squidge of crepe,
The hourly to-and-fro, occasional rages
If someone had taken one's place, a rape
Of customary decency, design to abort
Pregnant growth of mind before full period
By nerve war on another candidate for Mod.

Time Off

The Metropole's floor was hung on chains
And we danced there from ten to three,
Rising and falling to Delia Murphy's strains,
Her insouciant 'I'm a rambler, I'm a gambler'
Capturing us swaying, letting us go free,
The penultimate dance pulsing with gaiety.

The Gresham was for Saturday nights,
Decorous dinner dances from eight to twelve;
And then the sparrows clustered on the lights,
No problem of living that we couldn't shelve,
But no question of putting the world to rights
While slow quick-quick slow our pulses beat
Taking their time from our backsliding feet.

Maecenas

Virgil sat in his study, grinding out his epic
In answer to Maecenas' query 'Wouldn't it be nice if . . .?'
The imperative polite in his interrogative rhetoric.

Horace sensibly chose a more Epicurean topic
Relaxing with flasks of Falernian filled to the brim,
Thinking lazily under the shade of his fig tree
How lucky he was to have his lyrical time free,
Not to be celebrating the Emperor's propaganda whim,
Tracing to Trojans the benign world of his aristocracy.

Benign, perhaps, until Agrippina pointed to her womb,
Undaunted, saying 'Strike here, it bore a monster'
To her son's soldiers, sent under orders to kill her.

Urn Burial remarks that while Hadrian's horse got a tomb
Its wall-building rider's epitaph none can disinter.

Downhill on its long and varied way the *Pax Romana* went;
Everyone obeying orders wherever they were sent:
Only a lucky few received the Maecenas treatment.

The Daily Task

'Would you consider becoming, in September next,
Our Senior English master?' There could only be
One answer in my twenty-three year context:
That I had barely escaped, and was not yet free
From learning details, things uninteresting to me,
And to spend more time within these walls,
Passing them on to others, an idea that still appals –
Though for a moment or two I was perplexed
At how to refuse this magnificent offer
And not offend John Bennett's faith in me,
That led him, so very tactfully, to proffer
The accelerated beginnings of a career. He knew
My answer in advance: 'I'd say the same if I were you'.

Those Names

Those Greek names – Argos, Elis and Mantinea –
Suddenly recur without any reason.
They must belong to a far-off season
When learning such details mattered:
Who killed how many? When? Where?
What military power was shattered?

Though Elis was the home of Pyrrho
Who thought that nothing was certain,
Declared that none would ever know
True answers to questions set in train
By any philosopher's fertile brain,
T'other Pyrrho proved at Asculum
Such empty victories bring no gain.

Just to be certain some names can come
At random back into the mind again
Proves one Pyrrho wrong, t'other right,
For the victory of knowing one once knew
Those names – Argos, Elis and Mantinea –
Despite its being true, brings one no gain.

Front Square

My daughter, postgraduate, came from other places
(For Trinity wouldn't take a graduate's daughter
From the other island, because of some quota,
To read for Mod; such an idea caused laughter
Of an antisentimental kind), thought the faces
Were those to be seen in St Mark's Square,
Seen, overlooked, and some without an iota
That they strutted, exhibited themselves there
Like Yeats's goldfish, taking their petty stroll
Within the confines of a most translucent bowl.

ACADEME

E. H. Alton, *Latinist*

A Provost historians will describe
For official deeds or lack of them,
Short-legged barrel-chested Tubby.

Game? Rugby. Hobby? Carpentry.
An Ovidian, Fellow by examination,
Later a learned Professor of Latin.

Manner? Vague and at times, disjunctive,
Though sharp enough on a subjunctive
Or any crux or complex emendation
Of a manuscript or matter of taste.
Eyes? They belied any bumbling, alive
In assessing, most generous in humour,
In enjoyment, in observation of others
Who little knew how well he saw through
Pretence, foible, or inexactitude.

He gave his vivas with a roll
Of questions printed very specially
In an upward order, wound on a spool
He'd turned and fitted in a frame.
He spun the two knurled knobs
And the strip of paper snaked across
The polished wood to the examinee.
'The name?' He would say, glancing
At the gold watch he'd placed on the table,
Measuring out time's irrevocable loss,
For twenty minutes was all he allowed,
'Of this German scholar who was able
To emend *sota dices* to er – well, what?'
'*Nota dices*'. 'Good, good; hurry up, hurry up,
Only twenty minutes, you know'. 'Jahn?'
'Yes, Jahn, you're ahead of time; good, good'.
And so he turned the knobs, jotted marks,
Encouraged, fussed. 'You must know this;
Isn't it . . .?' 'Yes, it is . . .' 'Good, good, very good'.
So the absurd viva would jerk and flow along.

He loved the college, drew fragments of history
From sacks of papers he found in the Provost's House,
Liked to see Senior Fellows in place at chapel,
Enjoyed the college claret, himself most hospitable,
Benevolent to his children's contemporaries,
Amused to observe old flames' daughters
Repeating their mothers' flirtatious progress.
A radiance of delight, a lighthouse beaming,
He surveyed the shining faces of new scholars,
Offered everyone a chance to take a bearing
On his *humanitas* gracing a scholars' dinner.

John's Interview

The usual preliminaries: a moment to glance around
The table lined, each side, by unknown faces,
Chosen, doubtless, for views that were testedly sound;
Except for the professor, women filled all the places.
The Principal was brisk, no nonsense about her
('A lecturer is needed, so let's choose one, quick,
With all the expertise my experience can confer'),
Patently uninterested beyond labels, she was slick:
John could see why she appealed to the Civil Service,
And her authoritative voice matched her gong.
Over to the first square woman don in a trice,
Who also boomed: 'Was a man in a woman's college wrong?'
The professor winced with his twitching despair,
Asked about the book, about to be published,
Plans for research, what work-load John could bear.
His sensible role all too swiftly accomplished,
A tortoiseshelled woman took off her frog-like glasses,
Croaked out her minatory, hectoring demand:
'Will you give me a concise account, or what passes
For that, of medieval mysticism?' John took his stand,
And politely declined her query. 'Why will you not?'
'This is a post-Shakespearean post. Give me a day
To root in the British Museum and I'll then have got
Enough to answer you concisely; at present I can play
With the subject superficially (about which I know something)
But that, obviously, isn't what you want from me.'
She lapsed, muttering darkly about a refusal to sing,
In a diminuendo of croaks, about his unsuitability.
The Principal quickly assumed no further questions,
Added, as a matter of form: 'Nothing you wish to ask?'
He wondered aloud if he were – a mere suggestion –
To be appointed to what would be a pleasant task
Whether he could support a wife, let alone himself,
On the salary offered: did they help with housing?
Tortoiseshell blew herself up from her bosom's shelf,
Blood pressure rising too. The President's reply was rousing:
'We are not concerned here with such a thing
As how staff live or where.' She rose, too, from her chair,
And he left, thankful to breathe more wholesome air,

Having, luckily, a much more rewarding job abroad.
They later appointed – a characteristic witticism –
A person who's never written anything, a fraud
Most probably gorge-full of medieval mysticism.

Past History Man

This academic pads or shuffles round his cage,
Is regularly fed, usually ignores those who feed him,
Pretending his cage is the world, reserving his rage
For his fellows, those colleagues he attacks *seriatim*.
At night, of course, he roars defiance at the wide world
When he knows his wife, a former pupil, will hear,
Tells her how right he was, the insults he'd hurled,
Not knowing she no longer views him with respect or fear.
In his dreams he twitches, reliving all his busy day:
Two letters refusing students admission without reason,
An objection to make a professor's planning go astray,
And a card wishing an M.P. the compliments of the season.
To bring a new idea into a committee, he has learned,
Is to hang it sack-like for colleagues to bayonet,
So he now issues orders like a fierce sergeant,
Baffled, perhaps, that the sack is not at once upset
Since he's done his best to bring it promptly down,
Or, at the least, to have its main points overset
By referring it back, making it reconsider itself,
Arguing, in effect, its proposer is some academic clown,
But resenting a mere eyebrow raised against himself,
Cosily sitting there, for over twenty years, on the shelf,
None of his lectures altered in any way, no new books read,
Contempt for others' research echoing in an empty head.
He is armoured, heavily, like some armadillo,
Talks down when possible, invokes academic standards
He's never known nor understood, this punchinello,
Smug, stuffed with the windiest of all rewards
Since his unpunctured self-regard turns ever inwards.

Now

Οὐ μῆ and μῆ οὖ[1]
Miaow and bow-wow
What was he at
Playing dog and cat
With Liddle and Scott?
Lexicographical rot
Was his lot.
A four years'
Vale of tears,
Philological pressure,
Variant readings,
Lewis and Short,
A Senecan snort
(Not an amble),
Ciceronian clausulae
Sorted by Zelinski
In a study in Petersburg,
Sorted by Leninski
In an October revolution.
Four Octobers revolved
For him till he was free
Of examination –
His Classics are
Ancient History
Now.

---

[1] In English pronunciation: *Ow mey* and *mey ow*

Senate Business Committee

Three spires to see, eighteen other spikes or domes;
Beneath, slum houses, now departments' homes;
Victorian Gothic, Portland stone, reinforced concrete,
Tops of sycamore trees marking a former street.
This is the view from a stuffy new committee room.
Grave men sit round a table; new problems loom:
Less money, less space; more needs, more students.
All of this calls for deliberation, wisdom, prudence.
The light outside is brilliant; rainbow span
Between church steeple and the concrete ran,
Dispelling some of the solemnity and gloom,
As colour briefly beautified the stuffy room.

Brilliance

Francis, born to be a don (though he never became one)
Mastered erudite conversation, was witty in it,
Died without finishing any brilliant thing he'd begun:
Only a prolegomena man, friends were forced to admit.

Inside the Administrator

The tediousness of tidying
Just eats his heart away,
Knowing it will all silt up again
And make his calmness fray
Along the edges, where words collect
And ask for clean white paper –
Else thought, dream and poem, wrecked
Before their prime, cannot freely caper
Over the waves of time, confined
In his mind, that sorts, perforce,
Bills, circulars of the dullest kind
About some post or article or course –
Each envelope's a wooden horse
Ready to take him over, fully lined
With second-rate soldiers of administration
Toting brief notes, their tommy guns of annotation,
Cramping the captive mind in gieves of interpretation.
He leaves tonight; before the horse discharges
Its burnt smuts. His racing mind enlarges
Into a freer sphere: at last his desk is clear.

Scholarship

When your subconscious does its job –
If you've given it enough to ponder –
Things fall together, the hand grows bold
And seizes the book, that, for a wonder,
Leaps from the shelf to prove a point
And leads you further on to hobnob
With other books telling you things untold
You hadn't dreamed of, now conjoint,
Thanks to your subconscious ordering all
As if, momentarily, it enjoyed total recall.

Don Trefoil

From some sharp poems Don's composed
You might think he disliked a career
In which his forces could volunteer
To serve on all or any of three fronts
According to pressing need or whim.
Not so, no memory of pettiness blunts
The sharp sense of being a pilgrim
With a need to progress, to be opposed
As part of the intellectual to and fro,
Tension that plots the way that he should go,
Tapes paths through scholarship's minefield,
Plans advances by the administrative route
And applauds what pupils' victories yield:
The pleasure of having drawn them out,
Watched them learning what life's about.

Shedding

It is, he confessed, a strange sensation
To realise he need no longer keep
Those box files of lecture notes
With all their quotes and anecdotes.
True, they spend their time in sleep,
For he's never found any occasion
To use them a second time,
Believing that every lecture needs
New thoughts and its own treatment.
But just looking at them has sent
Shivers on an insistent climb
Along his spine, though now there succeeds
A sense of relief, equally strange,
Welcoming what their banishment will bring –
Blessed freedom from future lecturing.

Me and the Brother
(for Eileen Kamm)

I got rid of the brother I never had,
That academic doppelganger
Who wrote the books
That earned the cash,
Remaining a distant stranger.

Formal, even in his name,
He earned a little fame;
But shedding him made me glad
I could dodge the backlash,
Get rid of duty's hooks,
Whatever dragged him on.

My friends created him
In the image of their own desire . . .

John Bennett, trapped in situation grim,
Loving his barren, beautiful wife,
Found an alleviation of school life,
Of her irrational outbursts of ire,
In the subtleties of Plato's thought,
That war Thucydides refought,
And wanted me to share such pleasures.

Jack Storey, concerned with academic success,
Who'd turned his clever career into a mess,
Hoped I would rifle Trinity's treasures,
Win prizes, cut a dash in college.

There, classics imposed strict regulations:
The writing of Greek and Latin verse,
Loading memory with useless emendations
Till the circuits overloaded – and worse –
Left systems never to be trusted again.

Ho White and David Webb suggested discipline
Of another kind, refreshing a jaded mind,
Which a source-hunting regime could redefine,

Disciplined by classical needs, for objectivity defined
And proved, but breaking out of that narrow confine
Of the Golden Age into Yeats's wider romanticism.

Alton's encouragement opened Oxford doors, the hopes
That drove the brother into Bodleian's cool
While happily I played the social fool
Till Nichol Smith supplied the ropes
With which the brother bound me to himself.

He wrote the book: I did the drawings for it;
He lectured to the Dutch: I enjoyed the trains;
He lectured at Edinburgh: my oil painting kit
Lived at Glanmore, while I felt the strains
Of living on a quite inadequate salary.

Australia offered him – just thirty – a professorship;
What could I do but follow him gladly?
Gladly – there perhaps I could give him the slip,
Become myself again, tempted to use my oratory
(Taught me in the Hist) and become a public voice:
Creation without toil and ease on the beach,
Shagbeard and Sally Wester (1923 Rolls Royce).

The brother simply couldn't take my choice,
Too easy the Coonawarra – and man's – estate
Where stock exchange tips passed at each fete.
Even the difficult persuasion of Arts academics
Into creating a Research Council for Australia,
Winkling funds from US Foundations, didn't compensate
For leaving the academic task he'd set himself.
Here, most perversely, he felt himself on the shelf
While I enjoyed the future and its cornucopia.

His aim became living in the Yorkshire countryside
And writing *A History of Anglo-Irish Literature*,
But most wisely my wife helped to push him aside,
Knowing how much more I'd enjoy the wider allure
That London offered than any provincial peace.

So the brother travelled as doppelganger again,
Hitched to a journal's editor, British Council traveller,
Visitor to India, Africa, Europe, the USSR,
Who lectured in the US, toured Canada's plain,
Bringing dons, postgraduates – and money – to Leeds.

The brother, soon too world-besotted, demanded quiet,
But all he got was disjointed time for editing texts
Snatched from external examining, syllabuses, papers set,
Lecturing, tutoring, supervising, committees, the context
Within which he built that briefly cosmopolitan school
Where writers and scholars from most diverse places,
Each propelled by an invisible doppelganging-up brother,
Forgot they belonged to eastern and western races,
Made lasting academic friendships with each other.

Twice a year I sneaked away – a difficult feat –
Into the bookless bliss of Lédenon, using my hands,
Making new windows in twelfth century walls, mixing
      concrete,
Laying stones and then – something he never understands –
Doing nothing at all but gawp at the translucent sky
Watching swallows round the clocher, as they fly,
Twittering, swift-swooping in their unacademic arabesques.

I thought I'd escape him once and for all
Moving to Stirling: no administration, teaching only,
Colleagues with whom to collogue, countryside to enthrall.
He'd have to vanish here, leaving only Derry:
No A. Norman to the fore, not anymore.

He tricked me by lying low for just a while,
Lulled me into a peaceful false security,
Into thinking Wester Moss a permanent domicile.
Behind my back, no doubt with a cunning smile,
An editor again, member of A.C.G.B. and S.A.C.,
He was sure he'd turned the tables against me,
Even sat down and wrote that literary *History,*
Edited Yeats, and wrote a bigger *New Commentary.*

He laughed once I had built my drystane dyke
Transformed the midden into a flagged terrace;
Constructed a library and given Jeanne a pottery,
Made Bo and Mas a house out of the granary,
Confident he had not run his race, could efface
Such country pleasures, force me to use clichés
While he planned to continue his academic ways.
Two more books, he said, I really need to do;
You retire next year: how can it possibly affect you?

Desperate now, I try to blaze another trail
(These clichés ease my simple, rustic thought),
Tell him Derry writes poetry now, will live at Crail –
He laughs at the thought of another battle to be fought.

CREATORS

Cromlech on the Hill

Is the cromlech still there, surrounded by heather,
Grey, lichened, massive evidence on the hillside
Of pre-Celtic builder with time enough to wonder whethe:
The main granite slab could ever be persuaded to ride
Tautly on the lesser ones, once rocky earth was dug away?
To wonder, and then to persuade the necessary committee
Of lesser men his vision could indeed be achieved
Within the budget – biting back bilious rage at the delay
Created by niggling speeches of those who were 'worried'
About dangers of new construction methods, overriding
   overheads . . .
'May the Cromlech god strike them dead in their beds.'
He thought these words, but rehearsed them only to his
   patient wife.
Through vibrant passion this monument gained its still
   mysterious life.

Humankind Cannot

Nahum Tate didn't like reality much,
Took to improving Shakespeare;
Thought he needed it, that's clear,
By a most sympathetic touch,
Let Cordelia live in happiness;
Became poet laureate for his pains,
Bought himself a tuning fork,
Chummed up with Nicholas Brady
(Broth of a boy from County Cork);
Together they metricised the psalms,
Panted like harts for cooling streams.

Tate harboured in the Mint, seeking calms
After stormy creditors sank his dreams.
Dreams can pose questions as of right,
But how much reality can you bear?
T. S. Eliot asked G. Wilson Knight,
Who, playing Lear, dropped Cordelia
On the stage, on the opening night.

Boys from Kilkenny

Congreve was the luckier, for he had a father
Who had the wherewithal to fund him in London
After he'd spent weeks writing his novel in Shropshire.
Swift, like him a refugee from James's Tirconnel,
Had no one. His country refuge was Moor Park
Where Ménière's disease continued to earmark
Jonathan for inner noisy rages, the Philomel
Whom cousin Dryden would not recognise in him
Suppressed within Sir William Temple's dependant.

Congreve in London flirted with pert actresses,
Had Dryden give his play the fashionable cut,
Ungirdled lovely Anne Bracegirdle, to impress
The Town – while scholarly Swift wrote secret smut,
Having higher ideals but no hope of marriage.
Money mattered if one would be used like a lord
And he'd felt the need of that early in his life.
When a curate had dared to think of proposing to Stella
Swift promptly put him in his place. Could he afford
To keep her properly, he asked; was a carriage
Part of the deal? He asked himself would he transmit
That buzzing noise that seemed to herald in a fit
The madness feared by his fierce wit, his rational brain.
Despite his heroic reason, who can deny he loved
Who reads those desperate words he wrote to explain
The nature of Stella, unable to take the ceremonial
In the Cathedral next his Deanery, where her burial
Ended the long agony he'd known since she was ill –
Those earlier, windless days in dreary Holyhead
When poems dashed down all that could be said
In rage; impatient, kept away from her, made to wait
A passage to what he called 'the land I hate'.
Under no conditions was she to die in the Deanery,
He wrote, lest Dublin gossip sully either him or her,
Whose virtues he had sketched in playful praise
In witty, moving poems written for her birthdays
But whom (alas) he never saw alone. So rumour says.

True, Congreve fell out of love with lovely Anne
Who proved disloyal; he found instead a Duchess
Who bore his Duchess daughter. So rumour says.
He had a fuller life; success, then coronet's largesse
And the comfort of a close companion at the end
Voyaging to watering-places, still striving to mend
(What Jonathan had described to Stella so sympathetically)
The goutish effects of cheap and sour white wine.

Fastidious Swift died dirty, mad, locked up and solitary.

Immaterialism

The Bishop of Cloyne could not endure Romances
And he had a very great dislike, his wife said,
To contaminating churches with bodies of the dead,
So these should be buried along a walk of Death
Regularly planted with funereal Cypresses,
Where urns and monuments to those beneath
Could indicate the nature of human mortality.

'*The Finest Old Lady*'

Mrs Anne Berkeley kept her powers of mind,
Drew up *corrigenda* and *addenda* at eighty,
For Joseph Stock's life, published four years before,
Of his fellow bishop, who had left a widow behind,
Like himself most benevolent; and, what is more,
Her talk was sensible, facetious and lively.

Steele and Scurlock

Berkeley did not celebrate Steele
As learned and great
But he did permit himself to feel –
And indeed to state –
That he was the best natured man
And the most witty in conversation
That he had ever met.

Certainly Steele was most human.
When he was in very good company,
In a high state of intoxication
From drinking the health so often
Of the woman he loved best,
He was so completely overset
That he scrawled down a letter
To 'Dear Lovely Mrs Scurlock',
To tell her he was dead drunk
For her sake.

In every fat academic

No one has done a PhD on Robert Wilks
Who killed his man dead in a duel
(So inadvertently, clumsily, on stage
In some raffish Restoration comedy).
No one has weighed the witty fuel
He burnt in cartloads at a tender age,
Flourishing in faded theatrical silks,
Regarding rich life in London as a remedy
For the dim guttering lights of Smock Alley
(Apt excuse for sending his man to Shady Valley).
No one has done a guttering PhD on him,
Only the dim could possibly mix him
With his student friend Farquhar, that larker,
That rash stage-struck youth who really did it,
To the intense enjoyment of the Dublin pit . . .

By now the knowing-if-not-so-gentle reader,
PhD equipped, an Anglo-Irish special pleader,
Reaches for his gun, fills his breech-loader,
Realising that Charles Macklin did the deed
(In a London green room, not on Dublin stage),
Got off, although he'd done it in a rage.
'How *could* you mix them up?' Should Sean grovel?
No, he was dreaming not of a PhD but a novel,
Cries out, 'Don't aim your great gun at me',
Then screams, '*You* read it in *my* History.'

Doctors of Literature

Irish doctors dress the part from time to time.
Goldsmith bought purple silk small clothes, a cane
(Which came in useful later for the crime
Of striking Evans, editor of the *London Packet*,
Who'd called him an orang-outang, the swain
Of Mary Horneck, so rudely daring to bracket
Their names). He ordered himself a vast wig
And a scarlet roquelaure he could ill afford,
Hoping patients would be impressed by this rig.
His prescription for Miss Sidebotham become a by-word,
He declared he'd no longer prescribe for his friends:
'Only for your enemies then', said Topham Beauclark.

Goldsmith abandoned whatever skills – and legends –
He'd learned in Edinburgh and Leiden to re-embark
In the leaky ship of literature.

                                                    Lever, now,
Was different. While Goldsmith wrote of wild Oswego,
Niagara's thundering sound, Indians' murderous aim,
Lever, a newly graduated doctor, tripped his ego,
Thinking life after Trinity and Gottingen too tame,
Went to North America to learn the why, the how,
The when, and nearly the whereafter when captured
By one of Goldsmith's 'murderous brown Indians'.
Pinioned for death, he was mightily reassured
At the kiss of life conveyed by the Gaspé girl,
A princess, who slid her arms about him, his name
Whispered, his ropes undone by one skilled to unfurl
The wigwam's flap and guide him between the trees
To the Saint Laurence, escaping indigenous Canadians,
Slipping down the river canoodling at his ease,
Shipping a canoe as cargo when he crossed the seas
To launch his birchbark on the Liffey. The paddles,
The mocassins he wore gave a dash of romance
Surpassing much more orthodox props: those saddles,
Guns, rods, cards, and decanters used to advance
The rollicking Irish dragoon on his dashing career –
For Charles O'Malley, more than Harry Lorrequer,

97

Gave Lever his first success, got the cycle going
Of overspending and then, as income was slowing,
Of overworking to catch up.

                                Goldsmith all over again.
Thirty seven novels, 'marked by a lack of discipline',
Some tightly-scheduled tightly-tenured professors cry;
Disliking his early exuberance, they simply undermine,
As Yeats did, his achievement, calling it stage-Irish.
None of these fashionable critics seems ready to try
The later sardonic tales of the Anglo-Irish decline.
Neither approving nor appreciating the stylish,
They see these authors' generosity as an Irish fault.

Dr Goldsmith dressed the part, and Dr Lever too;
Their gambling instincts were most ready to assault
The public by extravagant display – Lever's fine horses
Drew him spankingly through the streets of Florence.
But the charge of overflowing hospitality runs true,
Uncalculating and warm-hearted in an ancient sense,
Easy-going welcome in all its bottles, all its courses.
Calculation never entered the changing part
Lever enacted in the hard-writing and hard-playing
Extravaganza that ended when he lost all heart
For writing, for living. There was no point in delaying,
Ill and lonely in Trieste, once his wife had died,
As his last Dedication declared in broken pride.

Another Irish doctor knew the virtues of role-playing
Practised in Dublin, after Vienna had added its tone
To Dublin's medical skill and a whiff of Oxford air
(Gogarty brought his wit and a barrel of Guinness there),
Then dashed past each patient-bearing kerbstone,
Driving himself into a practice, he explained,
To justify his flamboyant delight in showy choice
Owning both a Mercedes-Benz *and* a Rolls Royce.

Yeats denigrated Lever, Gogarty he over-praised,
But Goldsmith's sweetly humming hackwork in *The Bee*

Became 'the honeypot of his mind', succinctly phrased.
Goldsmith described how he sailed for Bordeaux
In the *Saint Andrew*: driven to shelter by a gale,
In Newcastle he was arrested and made to follow
Fellow-travellers, Scots in French service, clapped in gaol
With 'six agreeable companions' who'd come to recruit
More Scottish soldiers for the French. He languished there
Breathing, good naturedly, that noisome prison air
For several weeks, unable to prove himself no traitor.

The biographers, some distance on, find credibility
A strain, see Goldsmith, like Lever, as an inventor
Of overseas adventure. Smug in the sub-urbane safety
Of their burrows they can't believe a hare runs free;
Will they ever feel buffalo ropes constrain a limb
Or hear a gaol bolt slap snug into its socket?
Semi-detached, they cannot blink the fact that Gogarty
Dodged death, hoodwinking with his jacket
A republican hood, diving into a Liffey swim
That brought him, daring hostage, to the opposite brim.

These three doctors, abhorring any kind of vacuum,
Knew life as much as death to be imperious,
Dashingly different from their critics, so serious
In striving to bar them from literature's adytum.

Poor Dublin

Static June afternoon, pigeons overhead,
The rattling sound of a dredger clanking
Somewhere in the Liffey's languid flood,
Slums of the city lie festering; dead,
Unlike the brewery squatting on the mud,
Successful, like insurance, banking,
House agencies. Shaw was completely right
To cut and run across the Irish Sea,
To use his Dublin wit most seriously.
He saw it from gorse-covered Dalkey Hill,
This aged Dublin of the smoky haze,
Saw through it, too, with blue-eyed gaze,
Let his mother's teaching pay the bill
Until he'd written out his fivesome fill
Of fiction in London's fog and grime,
Then found an easier way to climb
Into the clarity he'd always sought,
Made theatre the arena where he fought
Against the stifling crime of poverty.

Gentle Readers

Harold Macmillan pronounced George Moore a cad,
Virginia Woolf wrote that Joyce was sordid,
Ricks and Davie shudder at Yeats's rhetoric,
Boswell, come to that, was envious of Goldsmith.
Administrators, authors, critics, and a biographer
All very clever, sometimes wrong, quite often right,
Some of them capable, too, of conveying delight,
Though quick to display their fastidious disgust
With a gentle person, a shy person, a landlord
And a jackeen who juggled words for them to read.

Young Turks

The brothers were poets. One, tall and thin,
Dressed elegantly, employing black or white
To emphasise cheek bones, jaw line, thin skin.
The other, short, muscular, built to fight,
Wore shapeless, grubby clothes indifferently,
Unconscious of his girth, rolling his eyes
As if to gather in a crowd, as if in ecstasy,
Though merely drunk and ready to surprise
An audience with some outrageous gesture
Of word or deed.

               The thin one loved hatred,
Rehearsed it in public readings, making sure
A republican heritage would be attributed
To his rising reputation in Irish-America:
The fat one loved love, thought hatred hateful,
Though utilizing, too, the dead republican da,
Whose savagery matched stories of Cooley's bull.

Mise Filid

It is wise not to offer whiskey to an Irish poet;
Whereas your lowland Scot takes his dram
Pontificating peacefully, his trewsered behind
Warmed by your fire, he seeks to cram
With every otiose detail recalled by his mind
Some anecdote whose drift he seems to forget,
Such his romantic Walter-Scottish love of fact.
Your highlander, though, I do not mention, for tact
Enters into it. But, glass and lips met,
The water of life flows fast down the throat
Of an Irish poet, to burn through accretions,
The debris of invasions, to release the inside urge
To relive the life of a *filid* – when potations
Followed a battle and the king could provide
Good meat, honey, bread – and perhaps a beast
As a gift if the poet's impromptus at the feast
Flattered his continuance of the sept's traditions.

Wood kerns stagger under their loads of logs
To keep the fire burning by the king's table
In the clearing, mist rising steadily from bogs
While the ousel and the blithe blackbird sing
Until drowned by the poet's reciter, well able
To outsing them all when he tunes the harp
And begins a lay well calculated to bring
Thoughts of lissome women, their hair sable,
Lips loving but of necessity sloe-sharp
When the water of life flows faster at table.
The poet lowers his breech, warms bare arse
By the glowing logs, thoughts turned to desire
By the inward fire that makes a mere farce
Of courtesy or devotion: for nothing higher
Than the waist troubles his unruly thought –
Except the risk that some sharp tongue
Of a sable-haired woman, who is not caught
In the web of his assonating verses, not stung
Into reciprocal passion, may make a mock
Of this ram, about to charge so blindly
At whatever ewe comes nearest in the flock.

In the morning his thoughts become unkindly
As he sees the shape-changers before his eyes,
Moving menacingly, eluding his bleary gaze,
And he decides to make certain of something,
Demanding yet another prime beast as prize
From the lowing herds of the king who pays,
As he always does, for fear of the savage sting
Of the poet's satire.

               It's unwise to start on whiskey
With your modern Irish poet. It's too risky.
When he declares he is a poet fear the worst!
It means he feels free, entitled to brawl,
To lie, to insult, to behave outrageously,
Shouting scabrous verses, quick to unshawl,
To unzip whatever woman's there to take;
And when frenzy mounts, impossible to slake
That thirst; he laments, strives to recall
The earls, mourns Gaelic civilisation's fall . . .
No patrons then would dare to default,
No one deny the poet his ball of malt.

Title Index

Index of First Lines